Mapwork 2

WRITTEN BY
Julie Warne
AND
Mandy Suhr

ILLUSTRATED BY
Damon Burnard

Books in the series

Mapwork 1
Mapwork 2

First published in 1992 by
Wayland (Publishers) Limited
61 Western Road, Hove
East Sussex, BN3 1JD, England

© Copyright 1992 Wayland (Publishers) Limited

All extracts of Ordnance Survey Maps are reproduced with the permission of the controller of H.M.S.O.
© Crown copyright.

British Library Cataloguing in Publication Data

**Warne, Julie
Mapwork 2
1. Title 11. Suhr, Mandy
372.89**

HARDBACK ISBN 0-7502-0302-1

PAPERBACK ISBN 0-7502-0516-4

Editor: Mandy Suhr

Designed and typeset by Matt Black dtp, Brighton
Printed in Italy by G.Canale and C.S.p.A., Turin
Bound in Belgium by Casterman S.A.

Contents

Finding the way	**4**
Where are you going?	**6**
Which direction?	**8**
Signs and symbols	**10**
Ups and downs	**12**
Find the place	**14**
How big is it?	**16**
Which map?	**18**
How far?	**20**
Looking down	**22**
Maps through time	**24**
Different maps	**26**
Trail around town	**28**
Glossary	**30**
Notes for adults	**31**
Books to read	**32**
Index	**32**

Words that appear in **bold** are explained in the glossary.

Finding the way

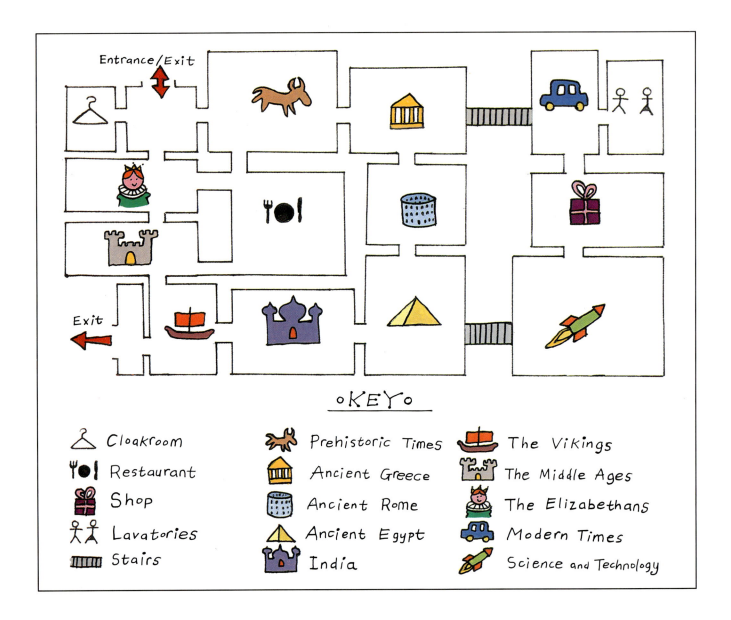

This is a **plan** of a museum. It is a view from above. It shows the area that the museum covers and the way that it is laid out. Plans like this are used to help people find their way around a place when they visit it.

If you visited this museum, what **route** would you take to get to the Egyptian exhibition?
How many different rooms would you pass through?
What would you see on the way?

Plans are used for different reasons by different people.
Architects draw up plans when they **design** a building. Builders use the plans as a guide to show them how to **construct** the building and how it should look when it is finished.

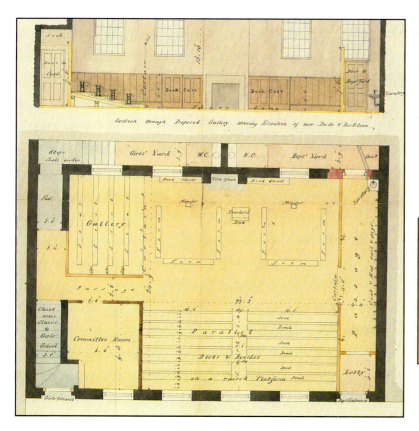

This is an architect's plan of a school that was built in 1870. Look closely. How do you think the school might have changed today?

Investigate your own school by looking at the original plans.
Has your school changed since it was built?

Where are you going?

Some people follow a route as part of their job.

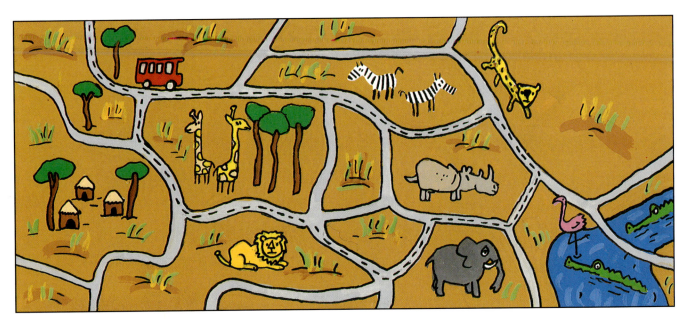

Ben is a **safari** driver in Kenya. He takes tourists out along one of these routes.

Jenny is a bus driver in Britain. She follows this route to take passengers around a part of London.

What different **journeys** do you make regularly?
Geoff has drawn a **map** of his route to school. Can you draw a map of a route you take every day? Now find your route on a real map. Can you see any differences?

If you were going on a journey that you had not made before, you might need to use a map to help you find your way.

Which direction?

We can use a **compass** to help us to find **directions**. The main directions on a compass are north, south, east and west.
In between these are north-east, south-east, south-west and north-west.
These can be used to find things that fall between two of the main directions.

A compass can be used to help find directions on a map. People who travel across country, away from roads and signposts, use a compass to guide them.

Help this mountain biker to take the right direction.

Which direction should she take to get to the hotel?

Which direction should she take to get to the lake?

Which direction should she take to get to the mountains?

Which direction should she take to get to the village?

8

Follow the correct clues to find the treasure.

Plan your own treasure hunt. Use a compass to plan a route around your school. Bury some treasure at the **destination**. Can your friend find it?

Signs and symbols

If you look around, you will see many different **signs** and **symbols**.
These help us by giving information quickly.
What do you think these symbols mean?

(see answers on page 31)

Symbols also appear on maps. They are used to mark buildings, roads and rivers, as well as giving information about places to visit and things to do.

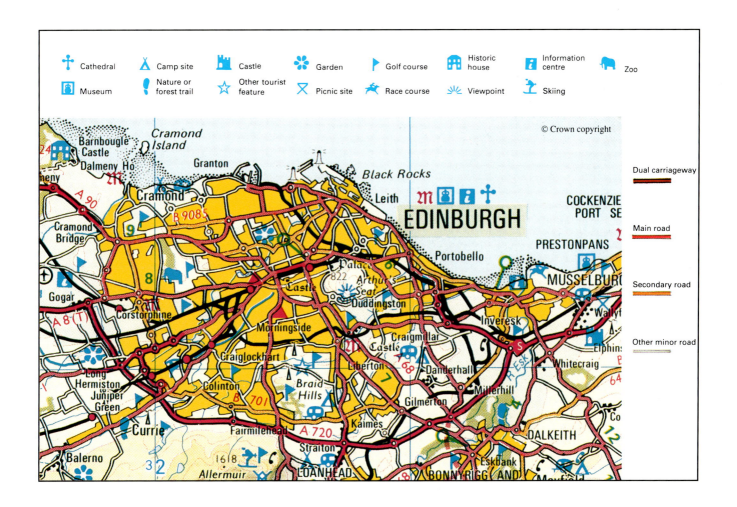

This is a map of the area around Edinburgh in Scotland.
How many different symbols can you see? Use the **key** to find out what they mean? How many different places could you visit in Edinburgh?

Make a poster to advertise things to do in Edinburgh.

Roads are shown on maps using different coloured lines. The different colours show whether the roads are **major** or **minor** roads.

Look at the roads on this map. Which do you think would be the busiest? Use the key to help you.

11

Ups and downs

Land that is shown on a map is not always flat. It has hills and **valleys**, high and low ground. The circular **contour lines** on a map show how the land changes in height.

Each contour line has a number which tells you how high above **sea level** the land is along that line.

When contour lines are close together, it means that the land is a steep slope.

When they are not so close, it means that the land slopes more gradually.

This map extract shows a part of the Peak District.

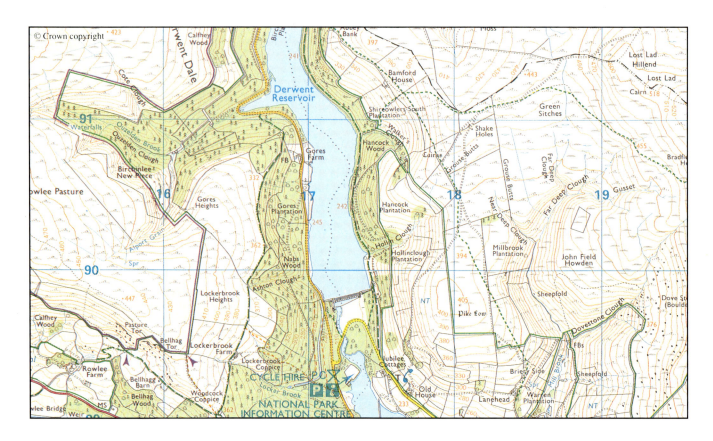

- Find the highest and lowest contours on this map.
- Can you find a very steep slope?

You can investigate the shape of the land shown on the map by making a graph.

Trace the contour lines from a **section** of map. Mark on how high above sea level the land is at each contour.
Draw a line across the centre of the contour rings.
Number the line at 5 mm intervals.

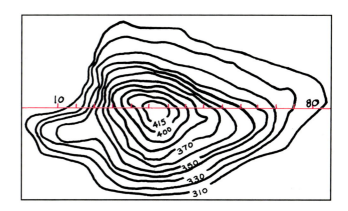

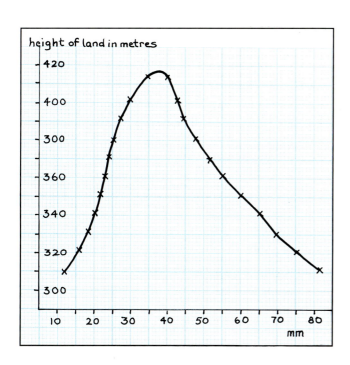

Plot a graph. Draw a **vertical axis** and a **horizontal axis**.
Mark height in metres along the vertical axis.
Number the horizontal axis at 5 mm intervals.
On your graph, plot the points where the contour lines cross the red centre line.

For example, at the first point, the height on the vertical axis will be 310 m. The point at which the contour line crosses the centre line will be 13 mm.

Join the points to find the shape of the land.

Use your map, graphs and trace to make a model of an area of land from plasticine or papier mâché.

Find the place

Grids are used on maps to help us find things quickly, easily and accurately. These two maps both show the same area.

How would you describe where to find the island on this map?
It is very difficult to describe the exact place accurately.

When the map has a grid you can use the **co-ordinates** to describe exactly where to find the island.
This island is in C3.

This is a section of an **Ordnance Survey map**. It shows part of an area of England called the South Downs.

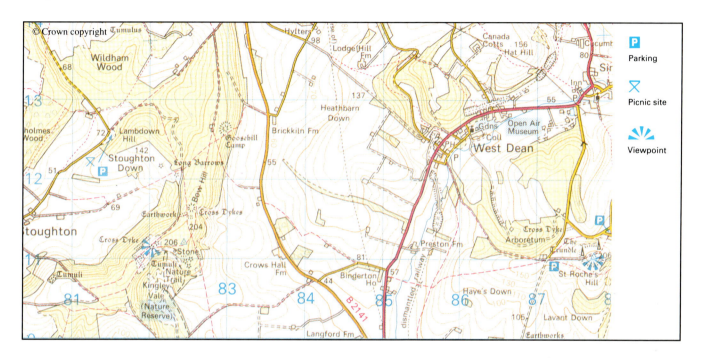

The grid is not made up of numbers and letters, but it has numbers along both axes instead.

You would find a picnic site at 81,12   You would find the museum at 86,12

- In which square can you find the highest contour line?
- In which squares can you find parking areas?
- In which square can you find a viewpoint?

> Use an Ordnance Survey map to plan a route for a friend around five places of interest. Give grid references.

How big is it?

These children are holding **models** of real objects.
A model is made to look exactly like the real thing, but it is much smaller.
It is built to a smaller **scale**.

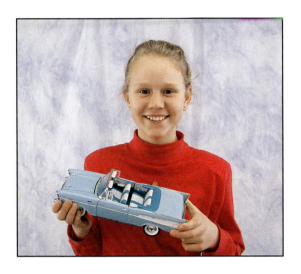

This model is one eighteenth of the size of a real car. The scale is 1:18. This means that the real car would be eighteen times bigger.

This model is one hundredth of the size of a real space shuttle. The scale is 1:100. This means that the real space shuttle would be one hundred times bigger.

When an architect designs a building, he or she builds a model to show what the finished building will look like. The model is built to look exactly as the building will look, but it is built to a much smaller scale.

Scale is also used when a map or a plan is drawn up. An area of land is drawn as it exists in real life with every building, road, forest and stream in exactly the right place. But it is all drawn much smaller so that it can be shown on paper.

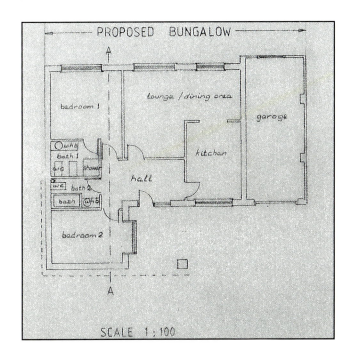

Different scales are used to show a smaller or larger area of land.
This plan of a house has been drawn to scale. It shows the area of land the house covers.

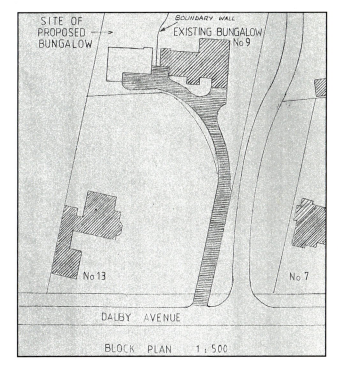

This plan shows the road in which the house has been built. The scale is smaller so that a larger area can be shown on the paper.

Investigate other ways in which scale is used.

Which map?

Different maps have different scales. The scale they use depends on the information that they are designed to give. Maps with a large scale show an area in detail. Maps with a smaller scale show a larger area.

These four maps all show the same holiday caravan park, but each gives different information.

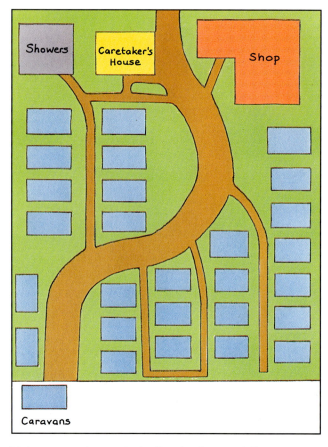

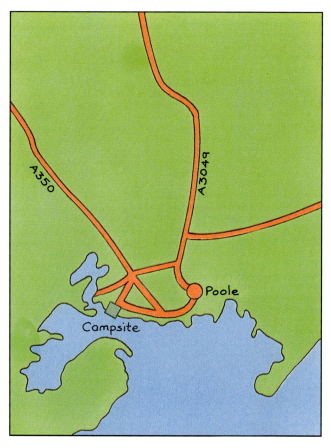

This map is a detailed plan of the caravan park. It shows where each caravan is situated.

This map shows the area immediately around the caravan park and the roads that lead to it.

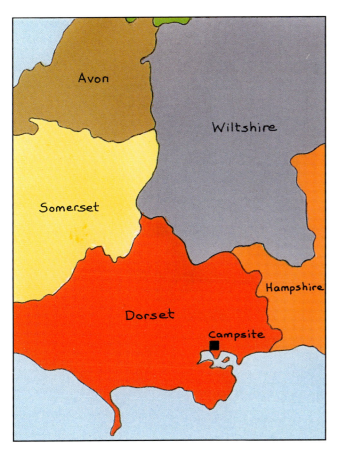

This map shows the county in which the caravan park can be found.

This map of Britain shows in which part of the country the caravan park can be found.

Can you map the place where you live in the same way? Use Ordnance Survey maps and an atlas to help you.

How far?

The scale on a map or plan tells the reader about the real size of a place, so scale can be used to work out **distance**, or the length of a journey.

This plan shows a shopping centre. It is drawn to scale so that when shoppers come to the centre they can see where each shop is.
The scale is 1:200. This means that 1 cm on this map is equal to 200 cm or 2 m at the shopping centre.
The distance from the entrance to the sports shop is 2 cm. This means that a shopper would actually have to travel 400 cm or 4 m to get to the shop.

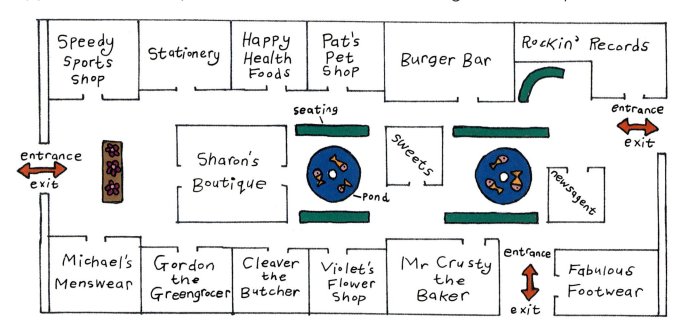

Jason has a list of things he has to buy. Locate the shops he needs to visit. Use a ruler and the scale to find out what his quickest route around the shopping centre would be. How far would he have to travel in total?

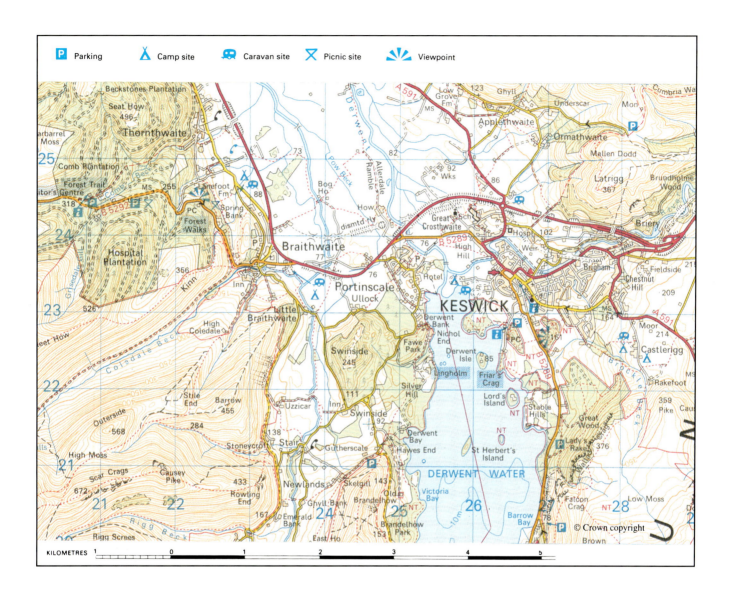

This map extract shows part of an area of Britain called the Lake District. The scale is 2 cm to 1 Km.

Imagine you are going on a camping holiday. You wish to visit four different camp sites.

Plan a route around four campsites, measuring the length of your journey between each.

What would the total length of your journey be?

Looking down

This **aerial photograph** shows a part of Caerphilly in Wales. What can you identify on it?

Can you identify the larger buildings? What do you think they might be?

Where are the **residential** areas? Why do you think they were built here?

Can you identify the main roads? Can you see the railway line? Can you find the castle?

22

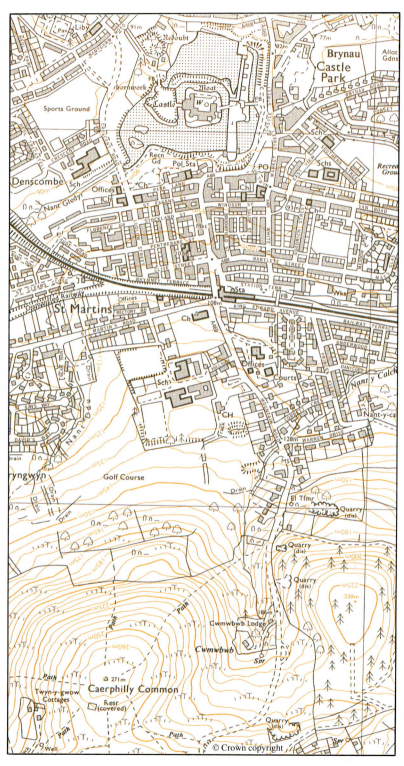

This is a map of the same area. What different information can you find from the map that you cannot detect on the photograph? Use the key to help you.

In what situation would the map be more useful than the photograph?

When would the photograph be more useful than the map?

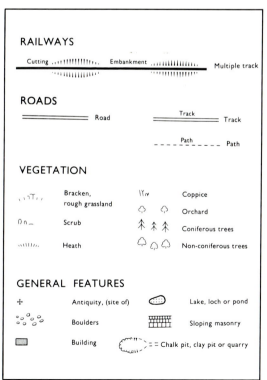

23

Maps through time

By looking at old maps, it is possible to investigate how a place has changed and developed over time. You can discover how the **population** has grown and where new roads and houses have been built. You can also find out what other things have had to be built.

Compare these three maps. They all show an area of Uckfield.

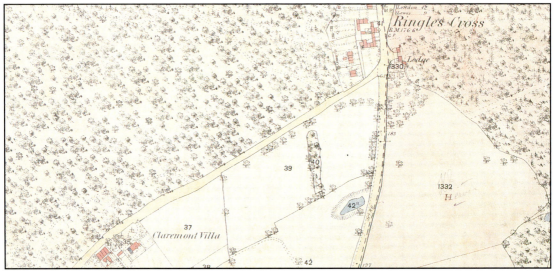

Map 1 shows Uckfield in 1874.

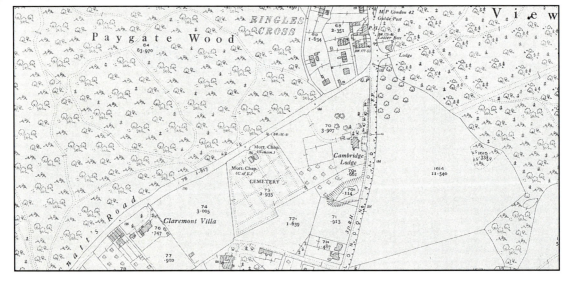

Map 2 shows Uckfield in 1931.

24

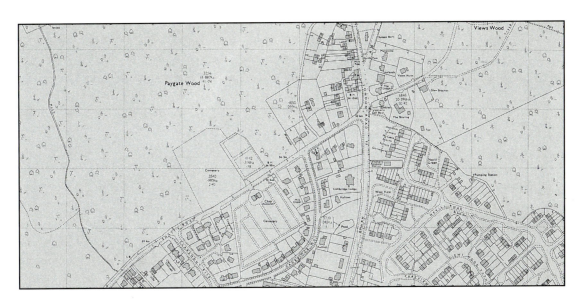

Map 3 shows Uckfield in 1991.

Look carefully.
What can you see that has remained the same in all three maps?
How has the place changed between 1874 and 1931?
Which is the London road? Can you locate it on the oldest map?
Why do you think the cemetery has grown in size?

Look at the names of the roads on map 3. Can you discover why these names were chosen by looking at maps 1 and 2?
Why do you think Uckfield has developed so much?

Research your own area. You will find old maps at your local records office. How has the place where you live changed over the years?

Different maps

Maps can be used to give many different kinds of information. These maps would not be used to find directions or routes, but they give other kinds of information.

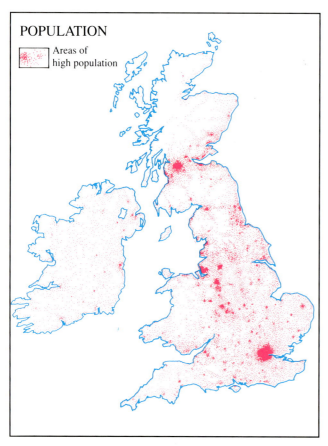

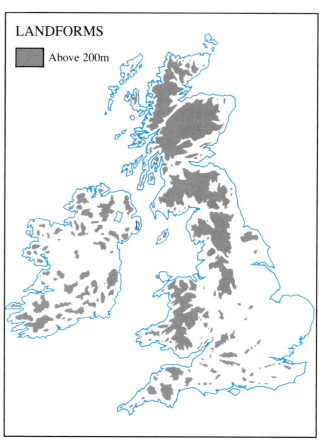

Map A is a population map. It shows where people live in the country.

Map B is a **landform** map. It shows flat and mountainous areas.

Compare these maps. Look at the key to help you.
Which areas have a large population?
What kinds of landscape do these areas have?
Why do you think more people live in some areas?
Why do you think fewer people live in mountainous areas?

This is a map of the world. It is designed to show where **endangered species** of animals live. How many different species can you locate? Which areas of the world do they live in? Use an atlas to help you.

Make a poster about animals in danger using the information that you have gained from this map.

Trail around town

Abi and Sam have been researching their local town of Brighton. They are collecting information to make a **town trail**.
This is a planned route which leads to places of interest around the town.

They have chosen to make a historical trail, as Brighton has lots of interesting old buildings. They have selected four places to visit on the trail, starting from the Clock Tower.

Using the scale on this map of Brighton, they have calculated the distance of the route between each place, as well as the total distance. They have used a compass to give directions, and listed grid references that refer back to the map.

They have put all this information together and designed a town trail pack.

The pack contains a map of Brighton, a booklet that they have written giving directions, and a tape which tells the listener about each place that is on the trail.

Can you follow their trail? Use their map of Brighton to help you.

With a friend, research your local area and produce a town trail. You may wish to make a different kind of trail, such as an activity trail around parks and sports facilities. You will be able to find lots of useful information at your local **tourist information office**.

Glossary

Aerial photograph A picture taken from the sky, often from an aeroplane.
Architect Someone who designs and plans buildings.
Construct To build or make something.
Compass An instrument used to find directions.
Contour lines Lines drawn on a map to show the height of the land.
Co-ordinates Letters and numbers which help you to find things on a grid.
Design To think up a plan of how something is to be made.
Destination The place you are trying to get to. The end of a journey.
Direction The way that you face when you want to travel somewhere.
Distance Measurement of space between two places.
Endangered species Types of animals or plants which are close to dying out because there are so few left.
Grid Horizontal and vertical lines making squares over a map.
Horizontal axis A line going from left to right.
Journey To travel from one place to another.
Key The part of a map which explains what each symbol means.
Landform What land looks like.
Major Important, large.

Map A drawing of all or part of the earth.
Minor Small, less important.
Models Small copies of objects.
Ordnance Survey map A map made by the official map-making organisation of Britain.
Plan An outline drawing of an object or place as seen from above.
Population The number of people living in a place or country.
Residential Areas where people live.
Route A course or pathway to follow.
Safari An expedition in search of wild animals.
Scale The dimensions of a picture, model or plan measured in proportion to the thing itself.
Sea level The level of the sea in relation to the land.
Section A part of something.
Signs Notices that give information.
Symbols A mark or a picture that has a special meaning.
Tourist Information Office A place where you can go and get information or facts about a town or city.
Town trail A planned route around a town.
Valleys Low-lying land between hills or mountains.
Vertical axis A line going straight up or down.

Notes for adults

Reading and interpreting a variety of maps is an important geographical skill which children need to understand and develop. This book introduces young children to essential mapping skills and concepts through a range of activities which develop their interpretation and enjoyment of map reading. There are also ideas for extension work with each mapping activity.

The use of maps is the principal focus of the Geography National Curriculum, Attainment Target 1: Geographical Skills. MAPWORK 2 follows on from MAPWORK 1, to continue developing these key mapwork skills and concepts into Key Stage 2, levels 2-5.

Pupils at Key Stage 2 should be able to:-

- identify features from pictures and photographs – homes railways, rivers, hills
- interpret symbols on maps and on a key
- measure direction and distance on a map
- follow a route on a map describing what features can be identified along the route
- use the eight points of the compass
- determine the straight line distance between two points on a map
- use letter and number co-ordinates; four figure and six figure grid references to locate features on a map
- extract information from large scale maps
- identify features on an aerial photograph and match them to a large scale map of the same place
- use different scales of Ordnance Survey maps – 1:50,000 or 1:25,000
- interpret relief maps
- extract information from distribution patterns shown on maps.

This book explores all of these skills.

Acknowledgements

Photographs supplied by: Geonex U.K. 22; Eye Ubiquitous 5 (top), 16 (bottom); Wayland Picture Library (Zul Mukhida) 5 (bottom), 16 (top), 17, 29.
Maps and plans supplied by: East Sussex Record Office 5,24,25. Ordnance Survey 11,12,15,23,25. © Crown copyright.
Artwork supplied by: Jean Wheeler 26; Geoff Noronha 7; Bob Suhr 17.
The publishers would also like to thank Sam and Abi.

Answers from page 10:

From top left: The Olympic Games, Telephone, No Smoking, First Aid, Cloakroom, Parking, No dogs.

Index

aerial photograph 22, 30
architects 5, 6, 30
atlas 19

Brighton 28, 29
Britain 6, 11, 19, 21

compass 8, 9, 28, 30
contour lines 12, 13, 15, 30
co-ordinates 14, 30

destination 8, 30
direction 8
distance 20, 30

Edinburgh 11
endangered species 27, 30

graph 13
grids 15, 28, 30

horizontal axis 13, 30

Kenya 6
key 23

Lake District 21
landscape map 26
London 6

models 16, 30

Ordnance Survey Map 15, 19, 30

Peak District 12
plan 4, 17, 30
population map 26, 30

road 10, 11, 17, 24, 25
  main 22
  major 11, 30
  minor 11, 30
routes 6, 7, 15, 21

scale 16, 17, 18, 20
school 5, 7
Scotland 11
sea-level 12, 30
signs 10, 30
South Downs 12
Sussex 10

Tourist Information Office 29, 30
town trail 28, 29, 30
treasure hunt 9

vertical axis 13, 30

Wales 15

Books to read

Keystart World Atlas (Collins. Longman, 1991)

Keystart UK Atlas (Collins. Longman 1991)

Mapstart Series, Simon Catling (Collins. Longman, 1985)

Mapwork 1 (Wayland, 1992)

Moving into Maps (Heinemann Educational, 1984)

Wayland Atlas of the World (Wayland, 1985)